Of Cured Light

Byron Dudas

BookLeaf
Publishing

India | USA | UK

Presentation by *BookLeaf Publishing*

Web: www.bookleafpub.com

E-mail: info@bookleafpub.com

ISBN: 9789363309869

First edition 2024

To my person, Anwyn

Thank you for always supporting me,

everything I do,

is for you.

Welcome In

When veins are roots.
They burrow within the body,
A constant.

They long to feed,
begging for blood and nutrients.
wrapping, reaching,
they squirm.

To establish pathways and shortcuts
throughout the highways of the body
they claw through cracks
tearing, poking holes.
To expand and absorb,
to transfer, and feed

My brain, a tree
now blighted.
with its branches twisted,
the blight commands brain to coil.
To choke out the healthy.
To keep from being pruned.

How can I stop the spread?
without losing parts of Myself

My health is at risk as my
veins still feed, this blighted brain.

Adrift

spill this drink
in open mouth
a floral
masked poison
weakness of mind
leads to
a headwater
a continued flow
every dam
be damned

I am driftwood now
wishing to be pulled ashore

Awake

Awake all alone
And struggle for warmth
An internal dialogue.

'Seasons change, and so must you'

To be left with,
A fluidity of personality
Happiness
A fluidity of fear
Distance

That creates,
A fluidity of struggle
Indifference
A fluidity of thought
Bliss

A stranger of the mind
Creates unstable-control.

'It flows from your slumber,
Sink in to forest's wealth
And reminisce'

To allow a soul and siphon
To disavow and breathe

'You have always been a part of this world'

Bogged In

slimy skin
a sign of sweat
left to grow

a new equilibrium.
it encases me,
I am castled.

this moat is growing
and I,
drown in
bog and algae

gates of body
closed,
in deceitful isolationism

and walls
newly made,
the sand and lime,
still wet
for
climbing moss and stunted tree
fill my joints
and
drink my swamped blood

Burned

bonded blood
rotten and tasseled
soaks through
this vessel of husks.
Its kerneled skin,
peels
from constant constriction
soggy
the heart still beats
in rhythm
as the husk
slowly absorbs
rotted bond.
saturated
the weight lops
in dances of colored pleasure
and skin dives for mud

revel in fresh shedded skin

Don't Resist

I sit and disconnect
but
electricity
does not yield

a whole world
newly spun

Neith
inside my head

her webs attract ideas
of spiders stuck
grief for benefit
from
goddess grace

for countless days
I breathe in false breaths
but
electricity does not yield
it makes me disconnect

Growth

duality of self
inside shell of skin
words are feed.
in swirls
connotations satiate
a struggle of hunger
in blood or in light
my conscious
is decided.
i weep in anger
and tense in kindness
wishing for my blood
to wash
clean

In Breath

Inhale
and ask it to be clean
Exhale
and wish for mind to dream

Inhale
when eyes are left as clouded screens
the mind begins to wander.
fears can grow if left unwatched
while time forever saunters
Exhale

Inhale
when bodies blood would start to slow
the heart begins to choke

Exhale
and bleed

In Decision

With,
dead dreams and poisoned purpose;
I continue to stoke this flame, abandoned.
the rain has since passed, leaving it's damp.
though there is no battlefield,   gear still lies.
I fear to enter these woods without guidance.
Without purpose,
 lost be the courage of I
 lost be the guidance of God,   I wait.
pleasantly
 the heart of flames,
Left to fold;
        an innate compulsion
Infection,
 found its footing, inciting a rot.
   I am at peace now
and now will I fold
   in order to grow; a symbiosis

mind—bracket—mold

In Discomfort

Southern dominions hug
in sticky stuck air
their exhales; hot breath,
oppress.
I pray for
small cubes of winds reprieve
but the goddess is limited in
this lordship.

I fear for
open heated hate
where tolerance is
a four letter word
and freedom is conditional.
bless my heart
and I'll join the hearts
hanging from the trees.

this land is screaming
but holy indifference is a deaf plague.

In Nightmares

I dream
and fall into a
emotional soundscape
familiar sounds
mix
and build
sound by sound
a monster
with emotional contexts
I fear
Its realness, its depth
without a choice
I spiral deeper into the layers of sound
picking out
and piecing together
the people
from voice
the guarded
from the
graceless
I weep

Neglect

It's rain again,
and we're left to sop in
a lifeless beauty.

the stick of cloth, worn thin
pressing, squeezing.
trying to warm itself from
the icy-ache of droplet's touch

distance
destination
and delivery.

the curse of tears.

we can huddle and hide within this timber
frame,
we can set up the stove, and stoke.

we can feel the heat,
but not the warmth.

for a shell of ice can encapsulate
even
the warmest of hearts

Perceived Publicly

here I lay
decayed
a busy day, left
my body with open pores

it plagues me
now
it seeps under my skin

this humanity

in growing density
it sinks
piling at my feet,

no longer can I
move.

I grow heavier
when will I fill?
and overflow

will I burst?

Rooted

the sap remembers
the taste of my skin,
I soak it in.
and skin retorts,
spinning its quick scars,
it spits in gums
stretched, and split
to chewed sappy scab.
blind tastebuds rise in bloods panic,
the spill of iron, the marriage of sap.

the sap remembers
the taste of my blood,
It soaks it in.
and the roots of false hunger,
gorge to gout,
a complexion sucked gaunt, and withered
now with growing density,
their hunger and mouths slow.

the body as husk,
I shed my skin
to collapse
to pile

allow my aid, and grow.

Spilled

I spill the light
it flows softly from my mouth,
cradles the sockets of my eyes
and bleeds from my ears

its luminosity breathes
in disbelief
it expels itself
slinking through the walls of my cells
I am river, waterfall, and moat.

Stewed

My mind spins, with the expectation of progress
i twist to furl my open skin, wishing for the
worlds calamity to calm
but it is within me.

An anger stews down into a scorched paste
my body a prison, each bone a cell,
i beg for freedom,
but my reality is laid out in front of me.

My eyes as lockets, to keep hidden
this false mirror that guides me
bleeds me
but I still draw breathe

Sugarcoated

In a ritual of remembrance, I bleed.
every thought and memory heads to the surface
and as they surface, I lay down my head.
bubbling, in dark raspberry-black welts
it won't be long now, till they scab over again.
I lay, candied in my past, a stiff enjoyment.
my skin heated raw, providing sticky-smooth
comfort,
I hold myself still.

And soon, as the flood cools, I am encased,
hardened in my life's blood, my lived memories,
and my eyes glaze over into false mirrors,

which birth my fears and regrets.
in distance, they take to the sky
and circle as vultures do

I lay sugarcoated
and wait for this new layer of skin

I stay still
and they are uninterested.
but if i move,
my fragile armor, my blooded shell

is sent to spiderweb,
and they will dive, to poke, and to rip.

I lay sugarcoated
and wait for this new layer of skin

To Be Loved

For the moon, full
through love
always must
give an ocean

Look to see,
a heart in harvest
a small lunar lover
wax with the tides
in a slow orbit

my blood-tide satellite
mourn me
though
every hope is weary
they are under
lighted water

For I shine

This star would rise through earth

A Heart Awake

I open, my eyes, to the darkest, of nights.
Or maybe, a morning, so dusk.
I enamor, with the sky, and the stars, on moonlit
mornings.
To feel, the wind.
To be a part, of the wind, I close, my eyes, and
cast off, the shell of flesh.
Forced out, to witness, passing gust, or breeze,
The morning, stars, gaze back.
Welcoming, attention, as they, sit back, and take,
turns.
Sparkling.
Reality is so close, If you allow it, to be.
Cast, off, conformity.
And sink too.
Asphodel.
Where river, and rot, both flow, and burn.
Reality, is so close, so. Wake up.

Death

do not kill
the ones that live
inside
for
death is
to be forgotten

and the pain of
remembrance
is secured immortality

Rebirth

an advance of velvet-tendrils
encumber the mind, embedding future thoughts.
soaking in,　　　bloodied.
exposed　red-winds
a forgetful protector forgotten.
Now,
blooming-stagnation
a festered fermentation
and organ–preservation
tendrils advance,　　　　　a spread of fuzz
　　deterioration; acid in stone

growth's requirement: sacrifice, of self
an alienation of attributes; minds presented
distaste
Overruled.

reform; growth of skin
　winding–whining　　　　　spreading-skin.

congealed consciousness

the tendril-fuzz amounts.
shaping-expanding control.
rooted.　old skin,　　　and

lost heart.

loss of being: begins.
                              now,
establish, cautious net of skin

for bodies blood, now a stone well
for fungled-fuzz to draw
 a full pail